An Awakening in the Sanctuary of My Soul

A Powerful Journey of Discovery Through Verse

SHARALEDON D. BRAVE

An Awakening in the Sanctuary of My Soul

A Powerful Spiritual Journey of Discovery Through Verse

Sharaledon D. Brave

ISBN (Print Edition): 979-8-35091-832-8

ISBN (eBook Edition): 979-8-35091-833-5

Table of Contents

MINOR

SAYINGS

Acknowledgement

To the myriad of loving souls who inspired me to complete this project, I simply offer my gratitude. Whether you are family, friends, an associate, or a stranger, I gladly acknowledge you as the catalyst for *An Awakening in the Sanctuary of My Soul*.

Writing this body of work was easier than the growth it took to accomplish it. I am fortunate to have friends who always see the best in me and encourage me to present myself fully through my art. To my brothers-in-spirit, Rick Grimes and Roger Phelps, I appreciate you both for being the gentle winds that lift me. To my dear friend and cousin Johnetta Meyers, thank you for being the earth that grounds me. To my friend and cheerleader Donna Satchell-Kimball, you've continuously been the water that nourishes me. Lastly, I'd like to recognize my godson and alumnus, Maurice Simmons, Jr., for being the fire that illuminates my heart, encouraging me to be my authentic self to the world. I am grateful to each of you for your energy, your support, and your commitment to my artistic endeavors.

Preface

This book
Would never be
Without first
Discovering me

MAJOR

BlackMan

There's more to the BlackMan
Than his charm and good looks
There's his wisdom regarding life
And knowledge gained from books

There's more to the BlackMan
Than his swagger and his style
There's his spirit that welcomes all
No matter his personal trials

There's more to the BlackMan
Than the media will ever show
There's his love for family and friends
That inspires them all to grow

There's more to the BlackMan
Than another BlackMan can see
A universal understanding
For each flows differently

There's more to the BlackMan
Than how he loves and trusts
When life throws him bitter fruit
He reconsiders and then adjusts

There's more to the BlackMan
Than malicious narratives
Being fully aware of self
Is absolutely imperative

There's more to the BlackMan
Than chains or bars will ever hold
Freeing himself of all constraints
As he consciously unfolds

There's more to the BlackMan

Little Black Boy

Little black boy
Born in a world so cold
Little black boy
Only a few hours old

Little black boy
With a grip so strong
Little black boy
To whom do you belong?

Little black boy
The years come quickly
But the gap of the classes
Leaves you alone and sickly

Little black boy
Starving for some loving
Still fighting for survival
Enduring the pushing and shoving

Little black boy
All hope is not lost
You can still make it through
Without the ultimate cost

Little black boy
Here, take my hand
It is my inherited duty
To help you stand

For you are a seed
With the potential to grow
What you will become
That, I do not know

Yet, I will nourish your mind
And structure your constitution
Here's to your life, my little brother
My small contribution

Son of My Soul

You are the son of my soul
The light of my life
You harvest grains of knowledge
And plant seeds of growth

You offer baskets of fruit
To be consumed by any
You move chairs and tables
To make room for all

You teach lessons of flight
With words and actions
Modulating thoughts and ascending
The realms of reality itself

You touch the shining crown
That radiates atop your head
You look down at your feet
For they are serving you well

You honor your heart
Whispering loving thoughts to your spirit
You rest in the wholeness of your soul
That your Creator forever guards

For You Are the Son of My Soul

Apple of My Eye

Possessing the strength of many
Along with the courage of few
The light of the Living God
Shines within and through you

You embrace the breath of life
Full of love and goodwill
Demanding mountains to lower themselves
And rivers to gently still

Your countenance whispers warmly
Inviting others to gather round
Encouraging those who are lost and lonely
To sustain until they are found

You are the hope of our ancestors
The celebrated son of elders
The glue that binds so many parts
With the skill of master welders

You share yourself as a living gift
That money can never buy
For these reasons and so many more
You are the *Apple of My Eye*

Daddy's Reflection

The beauty she sees,
Is the beauty you create

The trust she holds,
Is the trust you build

The love she feels,
Is the love you give

The peace she enjoys,
Reflects the spirit you are!

Beyond Reach

Reach for your son's hand,
And he'll give you his heart

Reach for your son's heart,
And he'll give you his trust

Reach for your son's trust,
And he'll give you his love

Reach for your son's love,
And he'll show you the image of God!

Papa Don't Cry

Papa don't sing no mo'
Now the angels sing for him
I can hear him in the breeze
As the leaves rustle in the wind

Papa don't hum no mo'
For the drums of life have ceased
He's moved to another consciousness
Surely he rests in peace

Papa don't laugh no mo'
But his humor still lives here
His fairy tales and storytelling
All I hold so dear

Papa don't smile no mo'
Cause he gave them all away
Preparing for the coming journey
He knew would be his one day

Papa don't cry no mo'
For the tears are mine to bear
Papa left me with a loving heart
And this is mine to share

BlackWoman

Beautiful BlackWoman
Daughter of the Earth
Sister of nature's wonders
Mother of priceless worth

You are the crown jewel
Shining its brightest tones
You are an ageless alchemist
Creating gems from common stones

Illuminating benevolence with dignity
With the majesty of an African queen
Imparting love and devotion
Void of spaces in-between

You nurse your historical hurt
And expose your present pain
You create sustaining substance
From a lonesome seed of grain

Presenting yourself complete love
In a manner you alone choose
Aware that there are little ones
Eager to walk in your shoes

Fully embracing your divinity
As the masses march in place
Charting your course with ready eyes
As you live your life in grace

Little Black Girl

Little black girl
Born with a spirit so strong
Little black girl
How will you get along?

Little black girl
With dreams of fairyland
Little black girl
Here child, take my hand

I will teach you compassion
For all God has made
I will teach you there is more to life
Than just making the grade

I will illustrate love
Through my relationships with others
That will someday assist you
In choosing to love another

I will teach you to reach
Further than what is at hand
And to fight for what you believe in
Firmly taking a stand

I will teach you to keep God
The center of your world
And that you are more than enough
Not just a little black girl

Being Me

I find myself stuck
in my own unyielding consciousness

The consciousness of fear and lack
The consciousness of *am I enough*
and enough for whom and for what?

I find myself searching for freedom
I didn't believe I would ever have
or deserve

I find myself locking doors
that I've allowed others
to close before and behind me

I find myself denying that I understand
what I know I long understood
Only to be a part of the crowd
who too, were as asleep as I, myself was

For to know that I understand
means only that I consciously, on some level . . .
maybe on all levels
refuse to take responsibility for the existence
I, myself have created

I alone may not have created it,
but I alone must change it
Change it by changing my mind, changing my
thoughts of myself
and my thoughts of others

It is only then that the freedom that stirs in me,
but not yet through me ... is ever free
I am only free when I discover the freedom
of being myself!

Love Lessons

I've learned to love
And I've learned to live
I've learned it's not about what I get
It's about what I give

I've learned that I will reap
Sooner or later, whatever I sow
I've learned holding on to old baggage
Will eventually show

I've learned that to expect true love
I must first truly love me
I've learned that a discerning spirit
Is greater than what my eyes may see

I've learned control should not be an issue
It's not about who will yield
I've learned that the only games played
Should be on a board or on a field

I've learned that love sometime hurts
I've learned it will always heal
I've learned that true love goes deeper
Then what I think I feel

I've learned that I can be patient
Giving others their desired space
I've learned that we can love one another
And not be in each other's face

I've learned to be grateful
For the opportunity to love
Fully embracing the energy
That we all are made of

Given

God gave me my voice
That I might use
To uplift others
Not insult or verbally abuse

God gave me my hands
That I might assist
Not batter another
With an angry fist

God gave me my feet
To run this race
Not for me to judge anyone
For their direction or pace

God gave me my eyes
That I might see
All the beautiful spirits
Daily surrounding me

God gave me my ears
That I might receive
Whatever I clearly hear
And choose to believe

God gave me my mind
That I might co-create
My life in consciousness
Not fancy fables or faltering fate

God created my soul
To experience this truth
To know this wisdom
Is my fountain of youth

Where Is My Love

Where is my heart
Does it reflect my soul
Is it showing the truth
That I'm created whole?

Where is my mind
Does it reflect my heart
Is it showing gratefulness
That I cannot tell apart?

Where is my consciousness
Does it reflect my growth
Is it showing my belief
Not some repetitious oath?

Where is my being
Does it reflect my Creator
Is it showing that our relationship
Only makes me greater?

Where is my love
Does it reflect my knowing
That love is not love
Unless it's authentic and showing!

When My Soul Awakens

What do I do
When reality is no longer real
How do I handle it
How does it feel?

How do I move forward
When what was . . . is now gone
How do I mend together
What seems forever torn?

How do I uproot
What was never planted down
How do I still the water
In which I now drown?

I start with being honest
Always with myself
Then I collect all the pieces
Of whatever is left

For within each piece
There is still divine breath
That keeps creating hope
Long after death

This Love

I will not hurt
I will not hide
I will not ignore
This love inside

This love that moves me
Protects me
Delivers me
Shields me

I celebrate this love
For its fullness
Occupying any space willing
To receive all its goodness

It is this love
That finds joy in my tears
I embrace this love deeply
That others may embrace theirs

I dance with this love
I touch with this love
I stand with this love
I am this love

The Power of Words

The sheer power of words
Has literally changed me
Into an enlightened being
From doubts and insecurity

I share my words
Not for form or fashion
I share them simply
For words are my passion

I am inspired by Divine Spirit
Scriptures and more
I write in stanzas of five
And lines of four

I embrace words with reverence
As you must clearly see
The best part of this relationship
That words, too, embrace me

They just keep on coming
To be written and combined
If it wasn't for words
I would've lost my loving mind

Work to Do

This is my work
My work to do
Not sit in judgment
Or criticize you

This is my work
My work to uphold
To open my consciousness
Grow and unfold

This is my work
My work to see
To tend to my spirit
And to better me

This is my work
My work to share
To spread it freely
Through the atmosphere

Within My Soul

I am the hope of my ancestors
the strength of my elders
and the wisdom of my children

I am the love
of generations before
and generations to come

I am the voice
that sing songs of freedom
and the momentum engaged in a movement

I am the conscience
that moves this country
and the dream that never fades

I am the pen
that never dries
and the paper that never crumbles

I carry this hope
along with strength
awashed in peace

Greater still ... I carry love
that carries each of us moment by moment
All within my soul

Who Am I

Who am I authentically
Do I really know
Am I who others see
Or is that just for show

Who am I genuinely
I passionately ask
Before I can answer
I must remove this mask

Who I really am
Is not about you
Who I am truly
You never quite knew

Who am I in truth
A reasonable question
I'm the expression of God
Embracing my human connection

If Life

Right in the middle of the word LIFE
is the word IF!

What IF I had done this or done that
Swung at every ball when my turn to bat?

What IF I gave love another chance
IF not marriage, a lifetime romance?

What IF I had chosen a better choice
Would I now have more reasons to rejoice?

What IF I'm grateful for what I'm given
Would I fully appreciate the life I'm living?

What IF I got rid of all the "ifs, ands, and buts"
Would I have the courage, would I have the guts?!

What if…?

Invocation

I invoke the power of Almighty Presence
To be present in my living
And to forgive me when I have doubt or fear
Or any careless misgivings

I invoke the care of The One
Who knows my nature by my name
Who holds me close and wipes my tears
And shields me from crippling shame

I invoke the goodness of The Giver
Who gives without regard
And if I think in lack or want
My mind My Giver guards

I invoke the character of Divine
To show me how to BE
To understand that who I AM
Is greater than what others see

I invoke the passion of The Lover
The Lover of my SOUL
It is this passion in this moment
My Being is completely whole

Testimony

Let my little light shine
Let it glow through the window and past the door
Let it shine to clothe the naked and feed the hungry
Comfort and embrace the poor

Let the words of my mouth
Bring a smile to someone's face
Let me take the time to say hello
And fellowship in flowing grace

Let my gifts and offerings
Leave my pockets full of cheer
Expecting nothing in return
For my blessings are already here

Use my life as a testimony
Through my actions, words, and deeds
How am I being spiritual
When I ignore another's needs

Forgive me for my second fruit
Be it my offering, talent, or time
With everything that surrounds my senses
None can I claim as mine

Let my tears flow freely
As my Creator moves through me
Nothing like my soul opening up
When I put all my trust in thee

When turmoil seeks me out
To the hills my eyes shall gaze
I will lift my hands and cry hallelujah
Caught up in the highest praise

What Mountain

Here stands this mountain
Perched majestically high
Its razor-honed crest
Sharply piercing the skies

This mountain stands fast
Obstructing my very growth
Couldn't go over or under
I know, I tried them both

This mountain stands solidly
Blocking greener pastures
This mountain, this rock
I must surely master

Standing in the distance
Even larger than it appears
Getting harder to contend with
From days to months, and months to years

One morning as I awoke
Singing praises of gratitude
Looked at this menacing mountain
With all its girth and altitude

Now I scale this very mountain
Reaching its highest peak
Believing I can manifest
Whatever I plainly speak

This mountain continues to strengthen me
As I squarely address my fears
For there is no mountain that is greater
Than my loving God that cares

Created to Be Loved

We were created to be loved,
thus we seek it all life-long

Looking high, searching low,
though never going deep enough
to the places we need to go

We fear going into the caverns
and into the crevices of our hearts
We fear crossing the rivers of our soul
and traveling in the dark

Thus abandoning the very essence
the makeup, the nature,
the genetic predisposition
of love itself

Love is bio-emotional
It feeds, it grows, and it reproduces
It shares, it feels pain, yet it heals itself

Love is much more than a feeling
It is a commitment to the universe
to invest your portion

It is commitment to yourself to grow
and develop, and to fully appreciate your existence
A commitment to others, to encourage them to
do likewise

Love, in its most basic form
is what makes us spirits
It is what illuminates us all
It is what makes the atoms providing life collide,
providing warmth and the glow that only love
can create

The very presence of love, much like a candle
in darkness,
has the potential to forever change it surroundings
Offering an open invitation,
to be redeemed at face value.
Love ... the most precious commodity;
Love!

Deeper Dialogue

What do you really think
What do you think you know
Are you watching love change
Or are you watching love grow

Have you been moved lately
In an unfamiliar way
Are you experiencing deeper feelings
Hoping one day they'll stay

Has your body been reacting
In ways strange and new
Is your reflection in the mirror
Showing a younger, more vibrant you

Yes, this is all you
With a far greater mind
The growth that you're experiencing
Occurs when the soul and spirit align

So, if all this feels deeper
Than you've ever dug before
Dig with greater passion my brother
You'll discover there's so much more

My Dwelling Place

You are my dwelling place
The sunrays upon my face
The wind against my back
The light between the cracks

The promise in times of storm
That I'll never be left alone
The anointing upon my head
By grace and mercy, I am led

You are my counselor
Touching my eyelids with sleep
You are my very best friend
For my secrets you do keep

You are my way-maker
When mountains are all I see
You are the gift of glory
Who sets my shackles free

When others try to trouble me
As I continue to run this race
I shall keep on keeping on
For you are my dwelling place

SoulMates

When my soul
cries out,
you are here
to listen.

When my spirit
is broken,
you are here
to mend.

When my mind
is racing,
you are here
to regulate.

When my body
is yearning,
you are here
to fulfill.

When my heart
was lonely,
you became
my mate!

Found

I find myself waiting
waiting for you
Waiting for you to show up
and be all that I imagine
in my morning fantasies

I find myself smiling
at the very thought of you
No thought in particular
None lesser or greater than the last

I find myself struggling
Overcome by the sheer power
of the magnetism that draws
my mind, my heart, I dare say
my soul to you

I find myself daydreaming
that this is the reality
I had bravely hoped for,
waited for . . . longed for

I find myself stretching my mind
like a fresh canvas
over a well-worn frame
that we might create whatever
we wish our present to represent

I find myself no longer wishing,
waiting, or wanting
I'm embracing the very best
that the universe has to offer
With a receptive heart
And a satisfied soul

I find myself ... found!

UnMasked

It is imperative
That we create spaces
Where masks are abolished
That disguise our faces

Showing our true selves
As Divine Love designed
Individually unique
Spiritually combined

As infinite divinity
Before time had begun
Stronger than silk
When united and spun

A weaving of consciousness
Unwillingly asunder
A foundation of greatness
Signs and wonders

We destroy these masks
Devised by this nation
Aware of our truth
As great works of creation

Don't Kneel on Me

We're still standing
We're still strong
We won't stand for an anthem
That is simply a song

We're still breathing
While air remains free
Yet publicly you murder
With the pressure of your knee

Where is the justice
For black and brown bodies
But you'll use us for research
For cures and antibodies

Black and brown bodies
Is all you seem to know
When you seek to enjoy
Sports, music, or a comedy show

Being fully aware
That we're so much more
You use political and economic power
To keep us begging and poor

An intentional, concerted effort
To maintain your status quo
You expect your privilege to be waiting
Wherever you decide to go

Never giving the slightest thought
Nothing is yours to take
Covering your deeds and assets
Claiming truth as lies and news as fake

Centuries of disrespect and disparaging remarks
That our psyches still endure
You look at us in wonderment
When we won't stand for it anymore

You murder our sons and daughters
Justifying the long-held hatred
Showing from the depth of your being
Money and power are all you hold sacred

The horror of countless lynchings
Bigoted masses surrounding a tree
Denying African-Americans any
semblance of justice
Let alone freedom or liberty

Lady Liberty can kiss my ass
For she never stood for me
She welcomes you to sit right down
But refuses to hear my plea

And Lady Justice can follow suit
With her covered crooked eye
Claiming she is just and fair
Is a complete and utter lie

So, don't be shocked or bewildered
When the pressure finally pops
This is what happens in America
When there are murders by racist cops

Chains

Drop your chains
Right where you stand
Don't mind the sound
As they loudly land

Step out of them
And then walk away
Regardless of what
Others might say

Make up your mind
It's your life to live
Many render advice
Not do what they give

It's amazing what happens
When the weight is lifted
You find yourself operating
In spaces you're gifted

Embrace this moment
Without the gravity of chains
Learn from your losses
Be grateful for your gains

Stand Up

Stand up for liberty
Stand up for just cause
Stand up for freedom
Stand against unjust laws

Stand up for our children
For our elders too
Our children are living sponges
While our elders guide us through

Stand up because it matters
Stand up because you care
Stand up because others stood up
That we might all be here

Stand up and stand tall
No matter your stature or size
The power you carry in your thoughts
The world will come to recognize

Stand up because you can
Stand up because you must
Stand up to show those who wander
Where you place your trust

Kick It Down

Ignore the door
That stands in your way
Kicking it down
Not tomorrow, but today

Don't ask permission
It's already been given
By the highest authority:
Your God that's living

You may try the key
It may not fit
Don't just walk away
You must not quit

Turn the knob
It keeps on turning
You keep on trying
Until your hands start burning

Go quietly within
And then be still
Then kick it down
With all your will

Dress Rehearsal

When the music starts to play . . . I'll dance.

When the ball is in my court . . . I'll serve.

When I'm up to bat . . . I'll swing.

When the door is open . . . I'll walk through.

When the window is open . . . I'll crawl through.

When opportunity knocks . . . I'm already dressed.

Woke

We must do more
Than sit here and dream
For while we're dreaming
Here comes another scheme

There's the age-old scheme
Another form of redlining
Pushing piles of documents to folks
Who don't know what they're signing

There's the other scheme
Of taxation without representation
And yet many of these citizens
Fought valiantly for this nation

There's the scheme of engaging
In multiple conflicts and wars
Brave fighters returning broken
Grappling with physical and mental scars

Then there's the mother of all schemes
Using property to fund education
Thus creating segregated schools
Then spending years in litigation

It takes so much more
Than simply being woke
The schemers are delegitimizing
The power of our vote

For the power of the vote
Is a mighty tool in our hands
To combat whatever weaponry
They have conjured up and planned

In This Chair

In this Chair...
Marriages are saved
Children are raised
Homes are bought
Lessons are taught

In this Chair...
Tears are dried
The young have died
The sick are healed
The promise revealed

In this Chair...
Children walk on stilts
Patches made into quilts
Recipes are shared
Wines are paired

In this Chair...
Fear is faced
Dreams are chased
Money is invested
Theories are tested

In this Chair ...
Communities are sustained
Generational curses unchained
Politicians held accountable
Hunger surmountable

In this Chair ...
Grievances are aired
Broken hearts repaired
Spirits are raised
God Almighty be praised

In this Chair!

Sittin' with the Sages

The spirit of Essex
Flows through me
Speaking his truth
Setting me free

The voice of Maya
Still rings in my ears
Speaking her truth
Since my childhood years

The brilliance of Langston
Leads me on
To explore other options
Not poetry alone

The fire of James
Burns in my veins
Calling out truths
And shouting out shames

The courage of Richard
Orders my tongue
To speak for the thousands
Of Negroes hung

The drive of Lorraine
Carries me on
To write about family
Struggling, yet strong

The eyes of Ralph
Exposes me
To the greatness within
That others might see

The lens of Gordon
Captures my soul
Freezing it, developing it
Presenting me whole

These great sages
Of literature and art
Having journeyed on
After fulfilling their part

Leaving a legacy
That must still be told
We create our own art
As our passions unfold

MINOR

Morning Matters

Be still and go within
Making each moment matter
Breathe slowly and deeply
To quiet mindless chatter

Wholly Made

I speak to my spirit
I sing to my soul
I hum to my heart
I am made whole

Manifestation

My soul got happy
My heart is relieved
My mind manifested
What I finally believed

The Offering

If you look around and notice
You're living in a mess
God offered you more
But you settled for less

Assigned & Aligned

When you are true
To your spiritual assignment
You can finally embrace
Your life in alignment

The Race

Here you are sprinting
To reach the finish line
Don't gauge my pace
It's your race, not mine

Morning Praise

Here's my morning praise
To get my day started
My mind's clear, my spirit's calm
I am good and open-hearted

Paving Your Path

Never mind what others think
Or what you've been told
When you create your own path
You pave your own road

Any Love

Some say I loved many
Others say I loved plenty
Knowing now what love is
I'm not sure that I loved any

Just Not

I cannot be angry
Bitter or hot
Because he just cannot give
That which he never got

The Marching Dead

I was a proud stepper
In the horde of the walking dead
Fully awake in my body
Yet fast asleep in my head

Willingness

I'm not afraid OF love
I'm not afraid TO love
I'm only afraid of being
Unwilling to love

Manhood

I am a man
And sometimes I cry
Brothas are suffering silently
While others are standing by

Spark

I am the spark
That ignites the flame
Full of love
Not stigma or shame

Generational Thirst

The longing for freedom and equality
Rises from the depth of my soul
A perennial thirst of every generation
Until the longing is made whole

Hidden Struggles

Before you run and hide
What others deem forbidden
Those who judge most harshly
Already have theirs hidden

Blue on You

Dear Georgia Governor
What do you do
When a solidly Republican state
Turns blue on you

The Feeding

Get outta your way
Come outta your head
Stop looping the lies
Historically fed

SAYINGS

Born and raised in the Lowcountry of South Carolina, I wholly embrace my Geechee culture. Though I am not fluent in the dialect, I cherish how we use "sayings" to express ourselves.

"Sayings" is loosely defined as the application of wisdom to formulate phrases to explain the simple, complex and messy aspects of life.

My maternal grandfather was a "sayings" specialist. Whenever I am with family members, sooner or later, the conversation shifts to something my grandfather once said. "You never know what goes on behind closed doors." is one of the "sayings" that significantly shaped my view of the world. The use of "sayings" became a way I would speak to myself about anything and everything, helping me to feel like my grandfather is still guiding me spiritually.

"Sayings" would later become a part of my writing, thinking maybe it would stick longer than any conversation. A man of few, but impactful words; it is he who taught me the power of authenticity and vulnerability, which would later shape my perception of love. I dedicate this section, "Sayings" to my grandfather, Charles Brave, Sr.

Passion

Passion occurs whenever I allow myself to be fully present in the moment that brings me pleasure.

Freedom

Freedom is where you find yourself
without fault, fear, or judgment.

Fulfilled

Life is never fulfilled by the people we know;
it is fulfilled by the people we love.

Courage

Courage is not the absence of fear;
it is the presence of faith.

Miraculous Adoption

You don't need a father, but I need a son.

Fearless Love

If only we loved without fear.

Self-Seeker

I am the man I always seek to be.

Hard Healing

That which is hardest to forgive
is that which needs healing the most!

Fit for Flight

Flight is impossible while sitting on your wings.

Wise Walker

I walked in quietly so that I disturbed no one;
I walked out silently so that no one disturbed me.

Achievement

I cannot achieve that which I am too afraid to lose.

Show Me

Show me how to do it
and I'll show you how it's done.

Commitments

Commit to a new understanding
of an old situation.

Poet's Pen

When a poet drops his pen,
another one picks it up!

Wasted Love

Love is never wasted.

Negativity

Negativity creates a hole that only love can fill.

Love Search

The most dangerous exploration of
mankind is the search for love.

Greedy Issues

The issue isn't that there's a lack of resources;
the issue is that there's an abundance of greed.

Acceptance

Accept that some people do not have the capacity
to fulfill the expectations you have of them.

Likable Love

Love 'em 'til you like 'em.

Dirty Sheets

If you only find your worth in someone's bed,
that's exactly where you'll leave it.

Freedom Song

Though you may deny the caged bird his freedom, you cannot deny him his song.